"With a unique ble
Clive invites us to c
The way he writes th
honest, gentle, profound."

Linda Allcock, author and co-worker with husband Jonty at
The Globe Church, Central London

"I truly loved reading *ONE*—it felt like I was being fed and pastored by a godly friend who had spent his life learning from and delighting in Christ. Every page celebrates the profoundly glorious reality of the Christian's union with Christ and how this knowledge brings purpose, power, and hope to every task, opportunity, and crisis of life. As each chapter concluded, I was left stirred to praise and draw closer to the Lover of my soul.

This book will help increase your enjoyment of the greatest privilege a person can know—to be one with Christ."

Tim Blaber, Pastor, Hope Church Winchester, and Director of Training for Commission Newfrontiers

"*ONE* takes complicated theology and lands it in your life. It takes the words of Jesus concerning union with himself and shows us what they mean for our discipleship today. Without quite realising it, we all too easily settle for a 'less-than' kind of Christianity. Written with delightful warmth and remarkable clarity, this book helps us see just how good and rich and full a life lived in union with Jesus can really be."

Steve Midgley, Executive Director, Biblical Counselling UK

"This book is a little treasure that deserves to be well-known. Maybe you'll discover it, and then 'sell all you have'! Clive Bowsher writes simply but deeply, like the apostle John. Bowsher mines John's Gospel for the essence of relationship with Jesus, and through the lens of union with Christ weaves stories of his own life—but it's the union of real-life intimacy with God-in-Christ, not something floaty. If you want a fresh vision of walking with Jesus day-to-day, then I encourage you to read this book."

Paul E. Miller, author of *A Praying Life, A Praying Church*, and *J-curve*

"Pastor-theologian and scholar Clive Bowsher gifts us with a beautiful, accessible, and biblical invitation to come further up and further into the mystery and marvel of oneness with God. Read this book and revel in the greatest privilege this world affords."

Simon Ponsonby, Pastor of Theology, St. Aldate's Church, Oxford, UK

"If you're longing for more reality, more buoyancy, more satisfaction in your Christian life, this is the book for you. Clive Bowsher presents years of his scholarship in this subject with enviable liveliness and humanity, so that every Christian (especially those struggling) can heartily rejoice in Christ."

Michael Reeves, President and Professor of Theology, Union School of Theology, UK

ONE

Being United to Jesus
Changes Everything

CLIVE BOWSHER

Union
Publishing

To my friends
Joel and HyeLim

CONTENTS

Connecting with the Real God

This book is about God's heart and your heart. It's about God's heart and my heart. It's ground where I want to tread with awe and care, because it's personal to him and to us. Being united to Christ is like that.

In some ways, I wish I'd been able to write this book twenty-five years ago. I'd probably have been spared a lot of pain that way. But I suspect I'd also have less of a sense of Jesus' utter goodness, and of his power in the midst of my human frailty. Where I've written about myself, I've wanted you to know the theology was learned not only in my study with Scripture open at my side, but also with many bumps and bruises, with tears, and in prayer.

Everywhere I go, I come across Christians experiencing what they would describe as a lack of reality in their spiritual lives. "God is out there, and I'm down here!" they feel. What's more, some churches seem confused about the difference that the cross and resurrection of Jesus make today. We live in an age which the New Testament tells us is the crescendo of God's rescue plan through human history, but we seem so unsure of what to expect from God in our here and now.

Many of us, in all honesty, are longing to discover, recover, or simply encounter more of the reality and closeness of God. We want to know this in our daily lives, our worship services, and our prayer times. As I said, this is special ground, and we need a reliable guide. Because we want truth. We want reality.

Jesus tells us nine things in John's Gospel that are possible *now* because of his resurrection—nine things which describe lives lived in relationship with him. "In that day," he says, "you will know ..." (John 14:20).

That day is now. It's today!

We're going to take a look at these nine "you will" sayings of Jesus. They come mostly in John 14–17, spoken after the Last Supper and just before his death and resurrection. They capture how the living God works today in the lives of believers. And they enable us to see how being united to Jesus changes everything in the here and now:

Love, Worship, Obedience, Nearness and Intimacy, Purpose, Life, Heaven, Freedom, Prayer.

Everything. Could there be anything more urgent for your life?

ONE

He Reaches Out

"In that day you will know that I
am in my Father."

JOHN 14:20

Philip's looking in the wrong place.

"Do you not believe that I am in the Father and the Father is in me?" Jesus asks (John 14:10). "I've been with you all for a long time now." There's something Jesus wants Philip to grasp for himself, to know on the inside …

Like Jesus, Philip is from the North, from Galilee. He's drawn to Jesus early on in Jesus' ministry. And Jesus has plans for him. Philip later becomes an apostle, one of the Twelve. He witnesses Jesus' ascension and receives the pouring out of the Holy Spirit at Pentecost.

But here in John 14, he's said to Jesus, "Lord, show us the Father, and it is enough for us" (v. 8).

That has always made me smile. Well, that would be enough, wouldn't it? Encountering the Father, seeing God. Knowing him, seeing him face-to-face.

Philip is longing for reality. He's longing for God. He's longing for something beautiful. Perhaps you find yourself longing at the moment too?

Philip already knows who likely has the answer. I guess he thinks Jesus will either grant his request (somehow) or tell him to wait a while (maybe a long while!). But Jesus gets Philip to change perspective. He tells Philip he's already looking God right in the eye:

> If you had known me, you would have known my Father also. From now on you do know him and have seen him. … Whoever has seen me has seen the Father. How can you say, "Show us the Father"? Do you not believe that I am in the Father and the Father is in me? (John 14:7, 9–10)

To know Jesus is to know the Father.

Seeing Jesus, the Son, is seeing the Father. That makes sense, Jesus explains, because "I am in the Father and the Father is in me." Or, as he puts it in John 10, because "I and the Father are one" (vv. 30, 38).

I grew up in a non-Christian family. God was definitely not in the picture. But I started to think Christianity might have something in it when I got to know some Christian friends at music college. I was on a gap year before heading off to university to study science. It was a time of change.

I still remember a lakeside holiday we took as a family that year. I had my books on knowing God with me, and I suppose I was hoping for something special. One day I went around the lake for a run, something I usually enjoy. The path was right by the water's edge. A few miles in, trying to bat away an insect, I managed to bat my own glasses into the water. Then, near-sighted as I am, I had to make my way slowly back to the hotel to get help … just to recover the glasses!

This seemed to sum up the frustration of the week. I needed spiritual sight, and I knew it. Learning things about God, by itself, was proving not enough. I wasn't reckoning yet with just how personal God is. Knowing him meant relating for real, and I had barely begun to do that.

I didn't need concepts; I needed a person.

Jesus' words to Philip in John 14 might surprise us. Here's Jesus, right in front of Philip—a person, a friend. Someone Philip can relate to and get to know better. And Jesus says, in effect, "As you see me, Philip, as you sense my heart and what I'm like, you're seeing the Father. I and the Father are one."

Not quite the answer Philip expected.

His mind goes back. He was having dinner with Jesus. To his surprise, Jesus got up from the table, took off his outer clothing, and tied a towel around his waist (John 13:3–5). He went to each disciple. He came to Philip. And he washed Philip's feet.

Jesus served him, loved him, and cared for him. And pronounced him clean. This is God, John tells us. You encounter Jesus, and you encounter the Father.

God's the God who stoops to save us, who isn't afraid to come down and help—and he's not afraid to kneel down with us either. We can relate to him. We can trust him. Picture for a moment Jesus cleaning Philip's feet, getting grime in the palms of his hands. Jesus isn't proud or overbearing—quite the opposite, in fact.

We're seeing God himself. The Son loving his people without holding back (John 13:1). The Son drawing near. The Father loving us the same way. We could never have dreamed God would turn out to be who he is and love us like this.

So, when you're seeing the Son, you're seeing the Father. (As the saying goes, there isn't a different kind of God lurking behind Jesus.) When you come to the Son, you come to the Father too (John 14:6–7), because Jesus and the Father are one. And the wonderful thing is that their love meets us with open arms.

Perfectly united

We get to listen to Jesus himself praying out loud in John 17. Twice more, Philip and the other disciples hear him say he is one with the Father (vv. 11, 22). "One" sums up so much of what John's Gospel teaches us—about who Jesus is and about how we can relate to him and the Father.

But we're getting ahead of ourselves a bit. Just what does Jesus mean when he says he and the Father are one? He has another way of saying it too: "You, Father, are in me, and I in you" (v. 21).

You-in-me-and-me-in-you relationship, he calls it.

This means when Jesus speaks, the Father speaks. His words aren't just his; they're the Father's. That's every word you hear coming from Jesus' mouth in the Gospels.

This means when Jesus does something, the Father does it too. He tells Philip the same thing (John 14:10–11). Just think of everybody you see Jesus relating to and everything you see him doing in the Gospels (foot-washing included). His words, deeds, and friendships aren't just his; they're the Father's.

When you see the Son, you see the Father. Their purpose and their relationship with each other even closer than we can imagine—perfectly united. One.

That's an awful lot to take in if we've not heard God described that way before. It is, without doubt, a dazzling kind of relationship that Jesus is telling us about.

Raising the bar on love

Tom, our pastor, was preaching yesterday morning. "We can overcomplicate the Christian life," he said. I nodded. "It's all about gazing at Jesus and wanting to be carried by, immersed in, the wave of who he is, the wave of Love himself."[1]

Now, admittedly, Tom's a swimmer, and we both live near a kite-surfing beach. You could change the metaphor, but Tom's right. "You can't control the wave; it's a lot bigger than you. God *is* love. Have you reckoned with the magnitude of this?"

Love is personal; it has to be. Surfing or skiing, music or hiking, art—all of these can be beautiful. (Perhaps not all of them to everyone, but you know what I mean.) Human relationships, on the other hand—personal and intimate and joyful ones—they mesmerize us.

But I think God raises the bar on love.

Imagine. The Father, Son, and Spirit perfectly united, perfectly one—before they created anything. Before galaxies or oceans, mountains or mammals. Before time and space. A world where everything was, well … right.

The Word, God the Son, with God the Father (John 1:1–2) and God the Holy Spirit, in the beginning. Jesus Christ the Son, "in the Father's bosom," closer than we can imagine to the Father's heart (see v. 18). A world

---

1   Sermon given at Grace Community Church in Porthcawl, Wales, on Sunday, May 8, 2022; with thanks to Tom for permission to include this.

where everything is right, and love is everything. The Father loving the Son at his side and glorifying him (17:5, 24).

Imagine that kind of closeness. That kind of harmony. The Father in the Son and the Son in the Father. Knowing each other completely. Loving each other perfectly. Loving with an intensity we can't plumb the depths of. It's the perfection we long for. Three persons, one God.

And the most astonishing thing—Jesus draws you and me into this divine life and love, into this dazzling glory (John 17:24). God is already drawing us into this beautiful love, to share it with him today.

Raising the bar on relationship

This God loves you, person-to-person. If we pause to consider, that's huge.

I don't know about you, but my approach to God can still sometimes be, well … too mechanical. I fall back into it. But I'd probably never treat a good friend that way.

Think for a moment about the struggles we can have as Christians. We seem confused about all sorts of things: worship, obedience, God's presence and our experience of it, mission ("Am I supposed to want to do this?"), even prayer.

But how much might be simplified if we made *relating to God* central? I mean *really* relating to him. Person-to-person. Sharing in the kind of love God has always been sharing and knowing, before anything was created.

Loving this kind of God is overwhelmingly beautiful. What if we made everything about joining in and loving God back as we enjoy the way he loves us too?

Our culture has cheapened love, and we're so thirsty. But Scripture says there is a deep river. Love which flows from within God, who is Trinity, from his relational heart to our heart—and then flows back to him and out to people around us.

Jesus teaches us that in the day following his resurrection (that's our day), we will know that he is in the Father and the Father is in him. The resurrection opens up the reality of the most beautiful love to us. It's stunning!

Everything flows from this Father–Son love, this *in-one-another* love, this me-in-you-and-you-in-me love.

Diving in

So, the Father, Son, and Spirit are one, perfectly united. And you're invited into the beauty of who God is. You're invited to live in this love.

If you ever get to hear Ard Louis talking about science and truth, you'll hear him say that deep truth can only be known by entering in and experiencing it from the inside.[2] Ard is professor of theoretical physics at Oxford University. He knows and loves Jesus. He's also used to problems which require a solution.

But knowing God isn't a hard problem for us to solve. It's a dazzling and thrilling reality to dive into.

We experience the real God as we trust him, receive his love, and begin to love him back. We dive in, and then we find the freedom of knowing the truth (John 8:31–32). If we wait for complete understanding first, we'll be disappointed (I know, I tried this for a while).

But when we relate to God, really relate, everything changes. Love, God's and ours, has the capacity to bring ultimate reality and the beauty of heaven breaking into our lives. "Love is the constant between our present, incomplete knowledge and the full knowledge yet to

2   Ard Louis, "Meaning, Evidence and Truth," February 13, 2020, in The Veritas Forum, podcast.

come."[3] Love is the bridge we need.

You can know and experience in-one-another love with the Son, a love so close it blows your mind.

When we hear Jesus is relating for real, loving us and able to reach us—today, in the here and now—we begin to realise that maybe we don't need to understand everything to love him back.

Jesus is inviting us to dive in.

Reflection

Let me encourage you to take some time out with God to reflect and enjoy being with him.

1. Imagine the conversation in John 14:1–11. What stands out to you?
2. Being united with Christ changes … Love.

Meditate on the words "God is love" (1 John 4:8) and the truth that he welcomes you in.

---

3   N. T. Wright, "Loving to Know," *First Things*, February 2020, 29.

TWO

He Relates

> "You will know that you are in me,
> and I in you."
>
> JOHN 14:20

My son's spiritual journey has been very different from mine. He began with God much younger. On Sunday evenings, he and I used to love driving into the neighbouring city together for "G&Ds and worship."

It was in that order just because of the time the G&Ds ice-cream shop closed! First time we went together, it was to celebrate his birthday. My friend Simon Ponsonby was on welcome at the church door. (I've just opened the book he gave my son that evening and re-read the hand-written message inside.)

What excited us (both of us) the most about those trips was going somewhere God was tangibly loving and loved. Being with people living in God's love and loving him back.

The bridegroom and the bride

You might never have thought about it this way, but God is wonderfully sociable. It's almost too outrageous and too stunning the first time you contemplate it—God actually wants us to know and love him. He doesn't need us to, but he delights when we do. He made us for his love.

Oddly, we find ways to dilute the joy. Sure, God is love, we think, but technically speaking. Maybe that's just saying how good God is. And us loving God, isn't that just the obedience thing?

But no, this is real relationship. The bridegroom and the bride. The passion we see in the Song of Songs. Loving, two-way connection. In-one-another love. Two-way love which, as we'll see later, is the very heartbeat of worship.

Two persons can't be as one, like the Father and the Son are one, without being close and intimately involved with each other. And you can't be united to Jesus without actually being in a relationship where you both love each other.

God talks about passion in Scripture for a reason. He wants you to know he loves you. He wants you to know he wants you to love him back. When we inhabit the beauty of that truth, all sorts of spiritual growth happens.

Leaping over the mountains

Christmas carol services (also after G&Ds) are another memory from that time. The size of the Christmas tree in the church left quite an impression on my son. The exuberance of his heartfelt worship in response to the carols made a bit of an impression on those standing near us! (Jesus tells us to come like children for a reason.)

What made an impression on me was hearing the minister talk on this verse: "The voice of my beloved! Behold, he comes, leaping over the mountains, bounding over the hills. My beloved is like a gazelle or a young stag" (Song 2:8–9). This was someone who knew intimacy with Christ—Jesus bounding across any and every obstacle in his desire to reach and befriend and love.

He's still doing that today. The God who is love is always relating to you, reaching out, leaping across, moving in your life. We can get so focused on theological boundaries and differences that we miss the essential—the love of Jesus. I mean being loved by him and loving him back.

Charlie Cleverly writes vulnerably about his own journey:

I encourage you to ask yourself if you are "fragrant" with love for God. Are you a lover of God? Would your friends … describe you as "one who loves God"? … You may be ever so orthodox on all necessary points, or you may have doubts you wrestle with daily, but have you learnt to love? … Are your arms wide open?[1]

Now, those can be deep and challenging questions. I certainly couldn't have described myself in those terms

1   Charlie Cleverly, *Epiphanies of the Ordinary: Encounters That Change Lives* (London: Hodder, 2013), 53.

when fumbling around at the lakeside on holiday. But I want to encourage you: if you're where I was then, it's possible to see a love which will awaken your love in return. It's possible to encounter Someone who will love you into life.

The flourishing vine

It's also possible to be around church and somehow miss this completely. But there's something better Jesus invites us into. "In that day," Jesus says, "you will know that … you [are] in me, and I in you" (John 14:20).

Now, hold on, you say. The Father and the Son … one … loving each other with beautiful, in-one-another love … perfectly united. I can see that. But me, united to Christ? Me and Jesus, one. Aren't we pushing things too far?

I want us to think about plants for a bit. Yes, plants! (Think David Attenborough on the BBC—don't switch off, or you'll miss something good). Jesus shows us a picture of a grapevine in John 15. Healthy and flourishing, complete with roots, trunk, branches, and bunches of fruit.

Then Jesus looks Philip, you, and me in the eye and

says, "See the branches and tendrils in this vine? That's you right now." He's the vine; we're the branching bits (John 15:5). Jesus and the people of God, together, one. A community of friends.

Jesus is the vine—he's clear on that (15:1). You can't find a place where the vine stops and the branches and tendrils start. That's you and him. You in him. Him in you. One plant, one vine.

Don't worry, Jesus knows his theology—he's not saying you're God or divine. But the union is real and has real effects. Jesus' life courses through the vine and produces fruit—genuine love in genuine community (15:5, 12). And apart from Jesus, people become like branches on the ground, dead and detached (15:6). But trusting Jesus—resting in his love and the promise he speaks to you—you're in him and him in you. You're united to Christ. One.

I'm struggling through my week; work is hard. This image of the vine comes to mind, and I'm reminded about the reality of being one with Jesus. There are real resources for the battles we face.

When Jesus explains this union in John 15, he explains it's all about life-altering, life-resourcing relationship.

Just as the Son is in the Father and the Father in the Son—remember that in-one-another love—so you abide in the Son and the Son in you. Loving, intimate, powerful involvement. That's how you and the Son are one, branch and vine. And the Father cares for the vine, tending and pruning it.

Let's take a look at the whole of the title verse for our first two chapters: "In that day you will know that I am in my Father, and you in me, and I in you" (14:20).[2]

The vine stands in the Father, so to speak. Christ remains in the Father always, and so we do too. That's why one of John's letters says that our fellowship and friendship is both with the Father and with his Son Jesus Christ (1 John 1:3). A friendship which allows John to say again and again: God remains or abides in you, and you in him.

As Jesus' words and promise sink in, we can rest. And resting in Jesus, the vine, you're in God and God in you. Think about that, wherever you're sitting or standing. That's true right now.

---

2   Jesus is describing spiritual, life-giving relationship here that is so close and intimate that each person is described as being "in" the other.

Jesus, then, wants you to know two things are true for you (15:1–12): you're clean (v. 3), and he loves you (v. 9).

Belonging

Many of us slip into worrying about not being enough for God, don't we? Not good enough or not clean enough or not special enough somehow. (We've spent far too long trying to get in with people who are just about as loving as we are.)

But we don't need to "get in" with God. God *is* love. And love overflows and reaches out to bring people in. We're asked to look towards the most perfect of loves. God wants to bless everyone looking to Jesus and include them permanently (John 6:40), to give them the gift of belonging. He brings us to himself.

You belong to the vine the way a living branch belongs to a tree. Not out of place, but in place or "clean" (15:3)—holy (that is, special and set apart) because you're united to Jesus, permanently. Not included as a concession. Yes, with some pruning and forming still going on (15:2), but that's normal for branches.

You're made to be there. Alive in his love. Belonging.

Not having to create an independent existence for yourself.

"Just as"

"Just as" is a powerful idea. "Just as," Jesus says, "I am in the Father and the Father is in me" (14:10; 17:21), those in the vine really can say, "I am in the Son and the Son is in me."

Just as the Son and the Father know in-one-another love, you and the Son can experience together the reality of close, in-one-another affection. The Father and the Son love you as their own.

That's why Jesus says, "As the Father has loved me, so have I loved you" (15:9), and "Father, … you sent me and loved them even as you loved me" (17:21, 23). In the vine, the love with which the Father loves the Son is in you. We're loved this way individually (15:5) and together. You belong because the Son belongs. "Just as …"

Let's pause for a moment. Everyday reality beautifully determined by the vine you inhabit: in the God who is love—Father, Son, and Spirit—and his love in you.

Being united to God changes the reality we're living. And so it radically shifts our perspective on worship.

The heartbeat of worship

A college student, believing the resurrection and the witness of Scripture, and, to my surprise, attending church! God had brought me some distance.

An evangelical church, packed to the rafters with young people and students. I figured I had come to a "worship service," but to this newcomer, the emphasis was firmly on doctrinal belief. Like most others in the balcony, I scribbled notes furiously. We sang lots.

But I'm not sure how much I loved. I'm not sure how much we knew ourselves to be in the presence of the God who relates and works in the here and now.

How central, I now ask myself, was true worship to what I was doing at those gatherings?

When we think "worship," we often think "difference." Different styles. Different music. Different sizes of congregation. Different denominations and liturgies (formal or informal). Different tastes.

How to worship on Sundays. How to worship during the other six days. Worship when we gather and when we're on our own. Even what we think the very word "worship" refers to. Isn't it strange how something which we instinctively know should unite us as Christians seems associated with difference? Sometimes it's just cultural and personality differences on show; sometimes, if we're honest, it's people's hearts.

Jesus says the key to unity is that we are in the Father and the Son (John 17:20–23). True worshippers trust in the same Son of God, the same Jesus, sent by the same Father.

So, let's do a thought experiment. Let's suspend everything usually associated with the word "worship" in our heads and see what happens when we make worshipping all about being one with Jesus. What happens here?

Now love comes centre stage.

Truly worshipping has always been about truly loving God with everything you've got, full on.

One day a scribe comes to Jesus and asks which commandment is first. Top of the list, most important. And Jesus quotes from Deuteronomy, "You shall love the Lord your God with all your heart and with all your soul and with all your mind and with all your strength" (Mark 12:30). In Moses' day and in Jesus' day and in our day, loving God is the most important thing.

Then the scribe says something. And Jesus agrees.

There's no one and nothing which compares to God and his glory. And so, to love him with all your heart, the scribe says, "is much more than all whole burnt offerings and sacrifices" (Mark 12:33). The mechanics, sacrifices, sermons, and songs of worship services mean nothing if they fail to revolve around loving God, full on.

We shy away from this for a thousand reasons.

I'd always been competitive. Straight-A student. Sporty, too, which helped a kid blend in as much as someone a bit different could do. "Achieving" hadn't come too hard over the years, and it seemed like value and identity I could build on, or so I must have thought.

Then a few things happened. I spent several months on my back with a viral illness. A great uncle teed off with me one day on a golf course near home but then never made it back. His heart gave out ... And I think something in mine broke that day too.

University came and went. I knew God was there, and I believed in my head that Jesus was raised from the dead, but I couldn't kick the habit of trying to earn everything, of trying to justify my existence, of trying to be, well ... valuable.

Somehow, I thought God would have preferred me

to earn his acceptance, if only I were capable of doing that. I wasn't sure I could like a god who ticked that way. To be honest, I was rather lost.

Tell someone like the newly graduated me to love God with "all their heart," and they hear "do better" and then worry how perfect the "all" needs to be!

I understand why you too might shy away from Jesus' words at this point. But I want to encourage you that there is a freedom you wouldn't imagine (and which I still sometimes forget) in this posture of true worship Jesus is talking about.

Vine talk

Remember our thought experiment. We're suspending everything usually associated with "worship" in our heads and making being one with Jesus central. We're seeing what changes when we make being in the vine central to worship. Now in-one-another love with Jesus becomes the heartbeat of worship.

"But I'm in the vine all the time," you say. We're remaining and abiding in Christ all the time. Aren't we always worshipping (our side of this two-way love)?

Thinking about marriage as pointing beyond itself might help here. My wife and I have been married for just over twenty-five years. I'm glad I walk through all of every week married to her. And that love and shared life, partnership and friendship, inevitably shapes my life in lots of different ways.

You'll be glad to hear we don't just coexist; we talk! Sometimes we're working to get something arranged or done; sometimes we're quiet in each other's presence. There are intense times and relaxed times. We don't spend every hour of the day in deep communication. But throughout the week, love comes to the fore as we dedicate time and space to one another. We don't want a marriage that lacks intensity in commitment or expression.

Now, my point here is, God wants marriage with us—it's a frequent theme in what he says in Scripture. Committed marriage. Intense and joyful marriage. On the other hand, I just don't think I'm committed to a heart full of love for God, bride-for-bridegroom love, if that passionate love doesn't come through when he comes into focus.

On Sundays, there's a space in the calendar where

God loves and blesses his people, his bride, in a special way as they gather. And we get to participate. We get to connect with, and hear from, him.

But we can forget he delights to hear our voice too (Song 2:14). He is, after all, the God who delights to relate to us.

Does sung worship together, or prayer, make up the whole of worship (on Sunday or other days)? No. But sung worship and prayer do allow our love for Jesus to come centre stage with intensity and beauty, and as a community too. The important thing is that it's happening, not how it looks exactly.

This love deepens as we express it. God is relating to us by his Spirit in the here and now—as we sing, talk, and listen. The call for me to worship is the call for me to sing to, listen to, talk to the Lover of my soul. The call is for us to love him and live to him, every day, with everything we've got.

One of the fun things about finding a close friend, or being parent to a child, is that you get to enjoy the uniqueness of that particular friendship. I don't think God wants carbon-copy worshippers. The Father is seeking children who worship "in Spirit and truth"

(John 4:21–24). Born from above by the Spirit and united to Christ the Truth, we get to express our love for the Father in a variety of individual ways. And I suspect God celebrates and delights in the variety too.

Loving him back

It's breathtaking, really—God actually wants us to love him back. He made us for this in-one-another love. He made us to be in the vine, one with him.

Everyday experience tells us that to know people, we've got to open ourselves up to them. Wouldn't you agree? We need to let them "see our face and hear our voice" (see Song 2:14 again). We might do that differently one-to-one or in a crowd—and each encounter might be different too. But there's a common thread.

It took me a while to cotton on to this: God is relating to me right now. I'm in his presence. It's 6:40 p.m. on a sunny Sunday evening at church. I know I'm looking to Jesus, in faith. I know I must be in the presence of the risen Lord, that he's relating to me, right now.

I look around me. There's a beautiful "fragrance" of worship, the sense that what's happening is being played out in real time, that God's not sealed off from us in this moment. We can reach him as we worship. I'm not sealed off from him; he can reach me by his Spirit. Even more—and this is sweetly overwhelming—God is wanting to love and meet us just where we are. He wants me to relate to him here and now, not in theory. I know I need to step out of my comfort zone (definitely an unsatisfying zone) and step into this close, dynamic love of God.

It's now 6:50 p.m., and the God who is vaster than the universe is coming up close. Suddenly, life isn't trivial. Perhaps for the first time, I figure God really does want me to love him back. To sing my heart to him, to turn my face to heaven without shame and in freedom. To open my arms to him as he opens his heart to me.

It was electrifying and often still is. Not because I was seeking some kind of experience, mind you. This was the end of a long journey through a valley to emerge into a new freedom. I was coming home, and the Father and the Son were already at home in me by the Spirit.

Was I going to sing? Yes! Did I care what people around me thought? Not really, but I wanted to be a help, not hindrance, to them. (I trust I was a help, as they were to me.) We prayed out, sometimes one at a time, sometimes together.

There's mystery, things we can't trace, when we relate to God in this way. We'd expect that. But is there also reality when we enter into prayer and sung worship, offering personal connection and felt love? Like so many others, I can say with sheer delight, I've found there is. There's a deeply satisfying beauty. And one which grows.

Reflection

1. Explore John 15:1–12.
2. Being united with Christ changes … Worship.

Picture yourself in the vine. A branch, alive and belonging. "Remain in my love," Jesus says. What an invitation, what a command! Linger and rest there. Worship there.

THREE

He Befriends

"I have called you friends, for
all that I have learned from my
Father I have made known to you."

"If you love me, you will keep
my commandments."

JOHN 15:15, 14:15

"Would you like to come too?"

I remember growing up in Hull with a great group of friends before relocating for my dad's work at fourteen (not a good age for moving house and area). There were always invitations to join in—with the ball games in the

45

back garden, the cinema trips, even the homework on the phone. (By the way, the "phone" was the size of two bricks. It would have broken if you had tried to take it outside. And the dial really was round.)

"Would you like to come too?"

"Yes, count me in."

My friends and I loved similar things. We played together and worked together. We even fought together when the opposing sports team looked five years older (but weren't). Of course, it wasn't perfect. We failed to understand sometimes. We let each other down occasionally. But mostly, we really had each other's backs. We pulled in the same direction.

And there was stuff you just didn't do. I had a friend, Richard, whose relative played rugby for Wales, and Richard was almost as big. Someone had set me up in a very unkind way one week. Then Richard stepped in, and it seemed never to happen again.

After the last end-of-year school assembly, everyone saw me off. Boy, was it hard to go.

Friends united

The vine in John 15 is more bunch of friends than

bunch of grapes (vine relationship, not vin rouge). You and me, together, united to Jesus in the vine—one.

As we've seen, the vine's held together at the deepest possible level. But who does Jesus say he's united to? The name he gives us links to what he wants us to do, but not in the way you might expect. It's not creatures, servants, or workers.

Sure, God created and gave you birth as a Father. (I love that—he shared his image with you and me; he put his life in us). But you're certainly not a creepy-crawly kind of a created thing.

Yes, the Son chose you to be productive, to love like him—to "bear fruit" that will stand the test of time (v. 16). But "servants" isn't the name he gives you, and "workers" won't capture it either. You're not on the outside receiving barked instructions.

You're on the inside, in the vine, let in on and brought into the Master's purpose and plan. And so, Jesus now calls you … "friend" (v. 15). A friend with the joy of being about what he and the Father are about.

Back in Hull we had a few teachers who were, though in a different way, almost part of the group too. (One of them even offered to have me lodge so I could stay at the school instead of move.) Jesus is certainly Master—but in his case, he's fully integral to the group. There's nobody like him. And he's setting the tone. He's showing us what's important here in the vine:

> "Greater love has no one than this, that someone lay down his life for *his friends*." (John 15:13, my emphasis)

Jesus has, I'm thinking, got Philip's attention again. "When you see me, you see my Father," Jesus has said. And now what we see is Jesus laying down his life for them (and us).

We can probably just begin to grasp the sort of love that might have us die for a loved one and friend. Love that's both human and beyond human. And on the cross, Jesus is doing that and more. By gazing at his love there, we're brought directly to see the Father's love for us. When you see Jesus, you see the Father.

This is how the Father loves you. Deep friendship. Deep love.

Spiritual crisis

I was haunted by that word "if" as I got further into working life. God would accept me "if ..." And I tried to fill in the blank. I really was a Christian "if ..." My salvation was secure "if ..." There seemed to be a lot of possible ways to complete sentences like those.

I had started out without God. Once he came on the scene, he was, well ... big, awesomely powerful. But I didn't feel I knew him very well. I didn't know what to trust about him. And I'd never even heard of being united to Christ (despite writing down an awful lot of sermon notes).

Worse, trying to make the grade had become a way of life. A way of what you might call "salvation," of finding value and purpose. It got me so far, but no farther. It wasn't very satisfying. To be honest, I wasn't very satisfying.

I remember a fortnight when I tried, seriously tried, to be like Jesus every hour of each day. My naivety was shown in the very real shock that followed. My sin went even deeper than I'd figured.

There was also a kind of culture which seemed to turn being a Christian into another hurdle to jump high enough to clear. The gospel (actually, not the gospel!) seemed like a legal contract—if I accepted the deal and worked hard, God would (begrudgingly?) cover my shortfall.

There was me and there was God. He was separate and to be reckoned with. But I couldn't see his face. We were not entwined in a vine. And I couldn't see his smile.

As the years ticked on, I got sick of asking the "if ..." question. I couldn't make it all fit together. I was taught I was justified through faith. And I was smart enough to see faith and obedience went together in the Bible. I felt I was being sent back to my own resources. I knew some true things about God and believed a lot of false ones.

I didn't like my version of God very much. And by my late twenties, my spiritual motivation had hit rock bottom.

I was in spiritual crisis. Lots of things contributed, I think. Poor theology. Church culture which talked about grace but shouted merit. My perfectionism at the time. But more than anything, I hadn't been overwhelmed by the person and love of Jesus.

My ill-conceived obedience faltered.

I needed to know that Jesus offered me friendship. Genuine participation and relationship with him.

Sharing with him. Joining in with something beautiful. I needed that, and he wasn't done leading me. His faithfulness and goodness didn't leave me.

Friendship fruit

Let's go back to David Attenborough, vines, and fruit for a moment. Please let's not miss the big picture Jesus is painting here. These branches, you and me, are fruitful when we're in the vine. When people aren't connected and woven into the life of the vine, all you get are dead branches (15:6).

Miss out on actual relationship with Jesus—living, breathing, loving, happening relationship—miss out on sharing two-way love with Jesus, and there just can't be any fruit (15:4). The friendship is the source of the fruit.

We all know that vines don't grow on grapes. Grapes grow on vines. So important not to get it backwards here.

Jesus makes you his friend at a deep level (deep for you *and* deep for him) and appoints you to go and bear fruit, forever (15:16). That blows my mind, if I'm honest. It also lifts up me up and makes me stronger, braver than I'd otherwise be.

I just need to remain in Jesus' love (that's where he wants me), have his words remain in me, and ask the Father for the kinds of things Jesus talks about (15:4, 7, 17).

And Jesus' word to you and me here is to be in the vine—in this two-way love, in this friendship with God—and to "love one another," as he loves us (15:12, 17).

Can I ask, have you and Jesus been building friendship for a while now?

So, what's the catch?

I can hear your brain whirring a bit at this point. Common purpose. Let in on the master plan for everything (15:15). Resourced. Full of joy (v. 11). Really loved. Hearing it and doing it Jesus' way. Obedience bubbling up because of him. Friendship fruit. God, really and truly … my *friend*?

If you didn't grow up with this kind of God, I understand. As you know by now, I didn't either.

"Okay," you say, "when Jesus tells me he's in me and I'm in him, and he intends me to remain there, there's definitely a special intimacy I share with him" (see

15:5). Yes. "When Jesus says he loves me as the Father loves the Son, defining myself as creature, servant, or even worker must be missing the mark" (15:9). I'm still with you.

"But," you ask, "if it's friendship fruit … what about God *commanding* us?" You might even push back and ask what Jesus means when he says, "You are my friends if you do what I command you" (John 15:14).

"If …" again?!

Not the sort of "if" you might be thinking, though. Let's consider this. You can tell an actual grapevine because there are grapes on it, right? It's like that. You can tell a friend of Jesus, someone abiding in Jesus (and Jesus in them), because they listen to his voice.

Jesus' face and presence are beautiful to them. They hang on his every word. And Jesus' words remain in them (15:7). Just as the Father's face and love are beautiful in Jesus' sight. And just as Jesus keeps his Father's commands and words (15:10).

So, Jesus says, "If anyone loves me, he will keep my word" (14:23; also 14:15, 21). It's friendship fruit.

There is *no* catch. Really.

We might be more used, nowadays, to thinking of

friendship among equals—mutual commitment, mutual honour, and similar status. Friendship with Jesus in the vine definitely involves two-way commitment and honour (with his coming first).

But friendship with the awesome, all-powerful One is more wonderful exactly because of who he is. More thrilling, and no less intimate—more intimate, actually.

Raising the bar on community

Remember the scribe in Mark 12? Jesus tells him that the commandment to "love your neighbour as yourself" is like the first one, to "love the Lord your God" with everything you've got (vv. 30–31).

"On these two commandments depend all the Law and the Prophets," Jesus reminds us (see Matt. 22:40). Nothing is more important.

Now, the vine shows us how they fit together—why the second one is "like" or "similar to" the first.

Remaining in the vine is enjoying friendship with Jesus. Participating in his life. It's having Jesus share the love of his Father with you.

Now, whoever you are, that melts you. It undoes and reconfigures you.

A few years back, someone at our church was telling a group of guys about the vine. Some of them looked pretty tough on the outside—rugby-playing, no-nonsense types. One of them, when he heard about the love of Christ, literally danced. Danced, wept, and laughed.

When you grasp it, loudly or quietly, life becomes about this love. It's all that seems to matter. And it just ends up spilling over to people in the neighbouring house, seat, or street.

Remaining in the vine is knowing Jesus sharing the love of the Father with you. Loving other people is you sharing the love of the Father and the Son with them. It's what Jesus means by obedience.

Aren't the voice and words of Jesus beautiful? "These things I command you, so that you will love one another" (John 15:17).

Suddenly, obedience doesn't seem a burden (1 John 5:3). This kind of life is attractive, even when it's not easy. It's shared—with Jesus, and with each other.

There's a lot of talk nowadays about community, how we lack community and want to create it. But the vine is different. Jesus creates a community which has a quality of love beyond our wildest dreams. Then he commands us (how sweet is this!) to remain in the vine, living our lives there and actually loving.

If we want more of this, "ask whatever you wish," he says, "and it will be done for you. By this my Father is glorified, that you bear much fruit and so prove to be my disciples" (15:7–8).

You're a disciple. Jesus is out in front. You're also his deeply loved friend, and so too are your brothers and sisters around you.

Beautiful obedience

So, please, let's not get duped about obedience. Dane Ortlund talks about a "disobedient obedience"—when it becomes all about behaviour. A bit like paying taxes to God when we don't want to, deep down. But heartfelt obedience isn't a means "to some other end."[1]

We can't buy life and salvation, not because we lack purchasing power, but because life and love are not for sale. After all, what sort of love from God would want to be paid for at the till?

God delights in blessing and giving. He *is* love. He enjoys friendship.

1   Dane C. Ortlund, *Surprised by Jesus: Subversive Grace in the Four Gospels* (Leyland, England: Evangelical Press, 2022), 52, 62.

If you're worried about the health of your heart (maybe rightly, maybe wrongly), can I encourage you? There really is forgiveness for every pain you feel at having grieved God. There really is love for every bit of brokenness you bring to him. And there's certain promise of fruit to come.

Let's explore and enjoy friendship with him.

Do you remember that fortnight I spent trying to imitate Jesus on my own? I wish I'd spent it instead in friendship with the Master of the cosmos who loves me. Would I have been listening to his voice and opinion on stuff? You bet.

Look to him. Remain in his love. Be in the vine. Ask. Trust him. Let him take care of the fruit.

Reflection

1. Read John 15:7–17.
2. Being united with Christ changes … Obedience.

Meditate on Jesus' words in John 15:7–17. Perhaps read them quite slowly. Experience him speaking them to you personally. Trust the promises here for yourself.

F O U R

He Comes Close

"You'll know the Spirit of truth,
because he'll remain with you and
will be in you."[1]

JOHN 14:17

I'm chatting in our living room with my dad (nearing eighty, but unfazed by technology). He's distracted by his tablet. We don't get to spend quality time with my parents quite as much as we'd like to nowadays, living at the other end of the UK as we do.

I find myself starting to feel a bit frustrated. My dad and I get on really well, but at this moment we're experiencing a lack of connection. I can't quite compete with

1   My translation.

the fly-fishing info (yes, fly-fishing) which is streaming across his tablet. If there was an emergency, I'm not altogether sure he'd hear me and jump into action.

He's present but he's not.

Perhaps that captures in a small way how you feel about God sometimes—present in theory, but not in practice. Not at all likely to react or interact with you.

Now, Jesus says something striking about God's presence in John 14. We could put it like this: being united to Jesus changes God's presence with you.

That might sound a bit surprising. (Your theological neon warning lights might even be thinking about flickering.) Jesus is preparing his disciples because he's about to leave this world. He knows he needs to comfort them with something real—and he chooses this promise of his presence (14:17).

He's going to ask the Father, and the Father's going to give the Spirit.

Jesus wants these truths, like all his words, to take root and remain in us (15:7). Let's listen in. We're this side of Jesus' resurrection. Jesus has asked, and the Father has given. Let's dive into what Jesus is showing us here.

Now or later?

He's been with his friends, his disciples, for three years. Now he's got to depart. That's where Jesus is at the start of John 14. (Do take a look at verses 2–5.)

He's about to go to the cross, where we'll see the beautiful, kind glory of the Father and Son written large.

He's returning to the Father's house, so one day we'll be with him there (14:3). In the family house. At home with the Son.

But here's the thing. There is a kind of experienced presence of God—the Bridegroom with his bride, being home—which we won't know until everything is made new (Revelation 21). But there's also a kind of experienced, loving presence of God, seen and known by believers now, which guarantees the future one. They're two sides of the same coin, Jesus says here. They go together.

And this means peace is possible now. Not a version of the doesn't-really-last peace that knocks around this world. Rather, it's the sort of peace Jesus has in relationship with the Father. And he wants his friends to experience it when he's physically absent.

Not being troubled. Not being afraid. Trusting him.

His peace is possible (John 14:1, 27). I often miss it. But I can find it by making space to enjoy the reality of his presence now.

Lost in the woods

Being separated from family can be terrifying for a child (and for an adult). When my wife was five years old, she went on a family trip to a local wood. She still remembers believing she knew the way back to the car and confidently setting out on her own. Suddenly, it was all trees and tears and the baddies she imagined lurking behind every bush!

Being reunited with family, by contrast, means security and a way to get home. It means familiar presence, both on the journey (14:18) and once you're there (vv. 2, 23). That's what Jesus is talking about here in John 14.

Now, you might say God is present everywhere. That's true. But he's not present in the same way everywhere, always doing the same things. God is only at home, present with us and loving us as he loves the Son, where people have come to put their trust in Jesus relationally. Person-to-person.

God at home

Sometimes I walk along the beach near our house. (For a year now, for the first time in our lives, we've lived by the coast.) The sea and the sky are large. Wild and beautiful. The space helps me reflect.

Sometimes I remind myself of these words that Jesus speaks to you and me in John 14. I need to remember the resurrection reality which he's shown me I'm always walking and living in.

Now, I want to be open about this. I've known times of intimacy with Christ which have breathed strong, strong waves of life into my faith and work. Waves which have astonished and renewed me, and brought delight. But I do still sometimes get swamped and disoriented by other things, needing these truths from Jesus to put me on my feet again. Perhaps you experience something similar?

We find it hard to live "in-between," don't we? After all, walking through the wilderness to a place full of life isn't going to feel easy (think Israelites— wilderness—promised land). But there are decisions to be made.

We can kid ourselves that the desert is great and try to settle there (weirdly, Israel did that back then, and people still do it today). We can even commit to the journey but mostly ignore God and his presence (that doesn't end well either).

Or we can commit to the unfathomable, personal dwelling of God with his people. We can worship in the wilderness, wonder at those pillars of fire and cloud, and walk home in, and by, his Spirit.

I've honestly known provision, encouragement, and direction by the Spirit of God which have more than astonished me, and which the world wants to tell me aren't possible. But God has taught me over the years that in the pressure, I can seek and know his presence.

How does Jesus describe this resurrection reality we're in?

Well, if you're trusting Jesus for yourself, he says, the Spirit has taken up residence with you (14:16–17). He is intimately involved with you. He is "in you." Yes, he's that close.

You're the place where the Spirit of God is personally present. He's at home with you. You can both relax and be in awe! "You know him, for he dwells with you and will be in you" (14:17). Dwelling in us not just together, corporately, but in each individual person too.

The risen Jesus hasn't left you alone. He's come to you (v. 18). As the Holy Spirit dwells with you, Jesus is present, powerfully and personally.

The Son and the Father love you and are at home with you (v. 23). You can't lose this. You can't stumble out of the Trinity's love.

This is the resurrection reality you live in as you walk along—you are in Christ, and Christ is in you. In-one-another love. Unbreakable.

As I walk along those cliffs, the most fundamental reality and truth about me I want to remember is: "I'm in Jesus, and he's in me."

Wherever I go, I'm in him. I can't lose his love. He's the world I inhabit. And wherever I go, he's in me. He's at home with me. I can breathe. I'm also in awe.

And he wants me to keep on enjoying intimacy with him. It's dynamic. (It sure isn't boring.) He's present to me, and I want to be present to him. I'm relating.

He's present and he's at work—I can't always trace it, but it's lively and beautiful and hope-filled. A bit like watching a dolphin slice effortlessly through the ocean, I sometimes see the ripples and sometimes I stand gasping at the leap out of the waves.

The reality you're living

John has a name for resurrection reality. He calls it Life (appropriate, when you think about it). People who put themselves in Jesus' hands enter life—the zone, we might say, where Jesus is King, the Spirit is given, and God's love-filled presence is known. This is what happens when we're grafted into the vine. It's, well …, it's alive—we can expect stuff to happen.

Sometimes when I'm asked to talk about being united to Jesus, I'll get this question: "Yeah, but being closely or intimately related to a person doesn't change my very being … does it?"

Even with human relationships, isn't it true that the "real me" is less sealed-off and more changed by re-lationships than we might think? My wife and I have been married most of our adult lives. We live "in" our marriage—it sets a context. It's a reality (I'm glad to say) and a dynamic. As people, we've shaped and changed each other in profound ways. Many of them we don't even notice.

Now, when you're intimately involved with God him-self, that's going to change the reality you live in even more. Think about it for a moment. The fact the living

God, Father, Son, and Spirit, has made his home with you has to change everything, doesn't it?

His Spirit is in you. You and he are intimately connected. Your lives are entwined. He's lovingly and powerfully at work (think again about the vine).

Your relationships shape you. "Me-in-you-and-you-in-me" relationship with the risen One changes the reality you're in—you're alive. So, expect to be surprised.

> "The world will see me no more,
> but you will see me because I live,
> and also you will live."
> (John 14:19–20)[2]

Knowing and tasting

The resurrection of Jesus changes the spiritual landscape dramatically. It changes what everyday people like you or me can see or know. "You will see me because I live,"[3] Jesus says.

---

2   My translation.

3   For the underlying exposition of John 14:15–31, an interested reader should consult the volume in the New Studies in Biblical Theology Series: Clive Bowsher, *Life in the Son: Exploring Participation and Union with Christ in John's Gospel and Letters* (Downers Grove: Inter-Varsity Press and London: Apollos, 2023). It's important to notice that two groups of verses in this passage, 14:15–17 and 14:18–21, are parallel to each other.

He's talking about people's inner selves and desires here in John 14:15–24. (He's definitely not talking about pure head knowledge.) The love you feel for him personally, wanting to walk in step with him and his words (vv. 15, 21, 23). A two-way love. God bringing his love-filled presence as he makes his home with us.

A tasting of the Spirit within. Knowing this Spirit, who is a companion like Jesus and who takes up residence with us (vv. 16–17). A deep comfort from him, as Jesus himself accompanies us and loves us (v. 18). Spiritual sight of Jesus. Jesus revealing himself to you (v. 21), for real.

We can water this down. But there's so much at stake. Jesus is alive, risen, present everywhere but offering to be present personally for you. With you, intimately. In power. In tender love.

The acid test Jesus gives us (vv. 23–24) is this: Will we, by trying to mould this into a different shape, risk losing a felt love and a personal presence which puts us on our feet, enabling us to walk with him?

"The wind blows where it wishes, and you hear its sound, but you do not know where it comes from

or where it goes. So it is with everyone
who is born of the Spirit."
(John 3:8)

Will we abandon our need to be in control, and live?

Entwined

Intimacy and nearness can be exhilarating. They can also be hard. As the Dutch worship leader Kees Kraayenoord recognises, "It takes the real you to step [further] into intimacy with the Father."[4] It takes trust.

David marvels in Psalm 139 about just how well God knows you and me. Each word and thought, before you knew them yourself this morning. When you'll lie down to sleep today, and how you'll feel when you do. Every day you're going to live out on this planet, before any of them has happened. That's intimate knowing. God knows you.

Even the very detail of how your body is knit together, intricately woven. A frame made in secret, but known to God. I'm known. So are you. If you go

4   Tim Hughes and Nick Drake, eds., with Liza Hoeksma, *Why Worship? Insights into the Wonder of Worship* (London: SPCK, 2021), 118.

up to the heavens, he's present there. If you were to go down into the depths of the earth, he'd be there too. He surrounds you.

If someone can know me so intimately *and* love me, I want to be known. I suspect you'd say the same. I want to be known and beautified by him. "I dare you to believe," Kees writes, "that God loves you so much that he actually wants to spend time with you."[5]

> We were sitting in a walled garden, a favourite spot, one autumn morning, sharing coffee and biscuits with some married friends. They're used to me reading quite a lot and then writing about it.
>
> "So, what are you working on at the moment?" my friend asked. I explained a bit to him about "me-in-you-and-you-in-me" in John's Gospel. About how churches in every generation need to grasp the truth of this. We were just chatting.
>
> This couple aren't Christians, but suddenly his wife (who doesn't know John's Gospel at all) suggests with a smile, "Isn't that pretty straightforward? I mean, understanding why he puts it that way. Sounds like a good marriage to me. Not knowing where one of you

5   Hughes and Drake, *Why Worship?*, 118.

ends and the other starts." (No, I'm not editing this conversation.)

Now, although good marriages between people aren't everything, they're certainly special. But imagine that kind of relationship with God himself …

The invitation of the gospel is Jesus inviting you to live in intimacy with him. Nothing can shock him. He knows you and he loves you. It's the invitation to know the reality of being one with him.

Come closer. God is inviting you to step further into his love for you, and to feel free to love him back.

Reflection

1. Enjoy reading John 14:15–31.
2. Being united with Christ changes … Nearness and Intimacy.

Try to put Christ's nearness to you into words, perhaps quietly but spoken out loud. Thank him for it. Thank him for the presence of his gentle Spirit with you and in you.

If you'd like to spend longer on this, turn to Paul's

prayer in Ephesians 3:14–21, using the words there to ask the Father for spiritual enabling to know more of this intimate love of Christ.

He Partners

"Whoever believes in me will also
do the works that I do."

JOHN 14:12

It was an unusual dinner party in Bethany.

Lazarus is there, for a start, and nobody could have imagined that a while back (John 12:1–2). He's now reclining at the dinner table (not bad manners back then). And that's still how it works today—when Jesus restores you to life, you get to kick back with him.

There's food, served by Martha, and chatter and the usual dinner party stuff. Then Mary, Lazarus' sister, causes quite a stir. Perhaps she's been looking at Jesus and Lazarus talking. She thought she'd lost Lazarus at one stage. She's overwhelmed.

Jesus really is everything. Resurrection. Life. Eternal life.

She notices again the love between him and her brother. Maybe they're laughing. Jesus' love for Lazarus, Mary, and Martha is obvious (John 11:5). These are three ordinary people, no doubt with all kinds of faults and insecurities. Yet Jesus knows them up close and loves them without holding anything back.

And Mary loves Jesus like Lazarus does. It's bigger than anything else. She doesn't care about the cost. She fetches a massive amount of precious ointment, made of nard.

And, literally forgetting herself and seeing only him, she anoints Jesus' feet with the nard (12:3). The whole house is filled with a beautiful aroma. Then, she carefully wipes his feet with her hair.

It's beautiful. Everyone is moved … Genuine devotion does that.

Then Judas Iscariot breaks in and makes a self-centred remark (12:4–6). But Jesus makes a cryptic one, which Mary must have overheard: "Leave her alone, so that she may keep it for the day of my burial" (John 12:7).

"No," we want to say with Mary, "this evening is all about life, not death." Surely it's all about worship, not suffering.

The next day, Jesus is talking to Philip again. And again, it's surprising: "The hour has come for the Son of Man to be glorified" (John 12:23). But the glory is going to involve his death, Jesus goes on to explain to Philip and Andrew.

The shape of Jesus' mission shocks us. The shape of his sonship isn't what we'd expect for the Son of God.

I think he wants us to recalibrate.

Mine or yours?

Probably some of their friends thought Mary had lost it! Lost her sense of proportion. Maybe even lost her self-respect.

But when someone doesn't care any longer about the things everyone else wants, it must mean that their love has settled somewhere else. Right? You lay things down when you've found something better.

Being united to Jesus makes everything else fade into the background by comparison. Loving this God and sharing with him is what you come to love. And, so, loving like him is what you come to want to do as well.

But being one with him has a certain shape which he wants us to understand.

Life as a pastor can be hard. My current work at a seminary involves helping people train and prepare to lead churches and to serve in all sorts of ways. I used to love ministering in a local church (and I love serving where I am now). But pastoring can be difficult, in whatever context.

It's a huge thing to stand where God is working and to be invited into the reality and intimacy of people's lives. And it's hard because love does cost.

When I first became a pastor full-time, Jesus' words to Peter were ringing in my ears: "Feed my sheep." Give your life, as I did, to feed and love them (John 21:15–17).

Now, believe me, that can hurt and cost in a thousand ways you don't quite imagine ahead of time. (So, if you can think of ways of loving your pastors back this week, please don't hesitate! They need you too.) It was the shape of Jesus' own ministry and journey too. Love is both costly and freeing.

One of the things that has sustained me most is having spiritual friends who understand gospel ministry from the inside, friends who have been involved with me in it and who partner, in the deepest sense of the word. (I also have wonderful friends who aren't pastors or elders but just seem to get it.)

More than once, another pastor made time, took a personal interest, and walked through a difficult problem with me because he'd walked that way himself before. They walked "ahead," and then they walked "with."

In a similar sort of way, I remember having tea and cake a couple of summers ago with a fellow minister and friend. He'd had a terrible morning, had got ill while driving to a previous meeting, and was clearly still feeling very shaken and physically weak. But we weren't embarrassed (as men sometimes have the knack of being). We wanted to talk. He knew without asking that I wouldn't see weakness the way the world does. We had a common perspective, and we shared a common desire to help people relate to Christ in all they do. In short, we trusted each other totally.

We helped and encouraged each other that day. He's a friend. A true friend.

God partners with you—in love and in what he's doing. He doesn't need to, but this is the way he does it. He delights to share his plans and mission with us, and to make this the experience of every Christian.

God the Son includes you. You're in the vine. And, as your friend, he sustains and partners with you there. He works in you and through you (think vine and fruit again). This is part of knowing "me-in-you-and-you-in-me" relationship with Jesus.

He walks the road again with you as you walk like him. He understands, from firsthand experience. He's gone this way before. There are shared loves and goals. Shared ways of working. And shared resources.

You might have noticed three little verses in John 14 which we've skipped over so far (vv. 12–14):

Truly, truly, I say to you, whoever believes in me will also do the works that I do; and greater works than these will he do, because I am going to the Father. Whatever you ask in my name, this I will do, that the Father may be glorified in the Son. If you ask me anything in my name, I will do it.

Just to remind us, Jesus has been saying, at this point, that he and the Father are one. Everything he's doing on mission to reveal the Father's love is also work the

Father is doing through him (v. 11).

Here in verses 12–14, it's the Son working through us.

We ask to do the kind of mission we see Jesus doing in John's Gospel (showing the Father's love). And he promises to answer and do that through us. He's working, so we're working.

The mission isn't just mine. (How could it be?). It's not even just his. It's ours, and that's both humbling and thrilling.

There's a lot that Jesus wants to do through us today. Particular places and particular relationships where Jesus himself wants to partner with you to make things happen. His mission. His power (his returned-to-the-Father power). It's all there in John 14:12–14.

My brother-in-law once bought me a book as a birthday present. It was full of examples of people who loved and trusted Jesus for real, and who took these words of his seriously. They'd laid down other stuff and, like Mary in John 12, decided that Jesus mattered more. It got me thinking. It got me taking seriously the words of John 14:12–14.

For years, I prayed these verses pretty much every time I went into a missional or a pastoral or a speaking situation. And I still pray them today almost every single time I preach. If I think Jesus would ask for something ("in his name"), I ask him to do it and show people his love.

Sometimes, if I'm under pressure and time's running short, I just say, "Lord, I'm praying 14:12–14"—he's used to the shorthand now.

"No one else can do this right now: it's you and me. I know you always come through. Thank you for John 14:12–14." And maybe, before the song ends, "Now's a good time, Lord. Do something special here. Hold me up and do what you want to do to show people the Father. Thank you for sharing this with me."

A sort of "over-to-you" prayer, in dependence on him. He always keeps the promise he makes in these verses.

Losing it

Jesus is answering our friend Philip again (and Andrew too):

Truly, truly, I say to you, unless a grain of wheat falls into the earth and dies, it remains alone; but if it dies, it bears much fruit. Whoever loves his life loses it, and whoever hates his life in this world will keep it for eternal life. If anyone serves me, he must follow me; and where I am, there will my servant be also. If anyone serves me, the Father will honor him. (John 12:24–26)

We've been seeing how Christ draws us into his love and calls us his friend. How we get to partner in the beauty of what he's doing and the beauty of his mission. The vine's a community with a love so strong that the world comes to see Jesus and understand the Father's love (13:34–35; 17:21, 23). That's beautiful.

A community of friends who know Jesus' presence and power at work through them. These are people who plan and pray to walk like Jesus. And who see him keeping his "I-will-do-it" promise of John 14:14.

Now, as Jesus talks to Philip and Andrew about his death here in John 12, he doesn't hold back, does he? Sharing and partnering in his mission involves a kind of dying too—otherwise there won't be much fruit, he says.

Journeying with him now and knowing future honour from the Father will require, he says, a sort of dying on our part. A losing. A laying down.

But this isn't a "grit-your-teeth and feel-worn-down" kind of mission. It's about love again (12:25).

Remember Mary at the dinner party in Bethany? When you think about it, she lost no more … and no less … than the financial value of the nard. Some (Judas included) could only think about the dollar signs. They were in love with their wallets. But Mary knows where she's headed. Jesus really is everything (and so the cost of the ointment pales into insignificance).

The choice Jesus gives us in these verses is real. And there's no middle way. (I wish I hadn't spent so much of my twenties looking for it.) Please don't hear me wrong—this is definitely a tough, fallen world. The cost of following Jesus is real. It's just that the cost of *not* following is catastrophic.

And love's what makes the difference. We could give everything we have to overseas mission (or anything else). We could even hand ourselves over to physical death. And still not gain anything. Here's the thing: *only* shared love with Jesus can overflow in genuine shared mission. The partnering is two-way.

If you love me, Jesus insists, you'll follow me where I

go. If you "me-in-you-and-you-in-me" love me, you'll follow me where I go (14:15).

These are real choices. "Just as …" the Father sends the Son, so the Son sends you and me (see also 13:16–20). And the world pushes back. Sometimes it pushes back hard. At that point, we need to remember it did the same thing to Jesus. It's a reassuring reminder that we belong to him (15:19).

I'm writing this chapter in Stockholm, a city we've visited throughout our married lives (My mother-in-law grew up just south of here).

I'm nearing fifty now. I'm thinking about what laying things down and partnering with Jesus has been like. What losing things has been like, in all honesty.

Love does indeed drive decisions and priorities. To take just one example, after about twelve years of being married, we were used to our freedom as a couple. But my wife was longing to have a child. At the time, I really wasn't so sure. But I could see how she felt about this. In the end, it didn't feel like a decision, but like the only natural response. What I'm saying here is that loving her made other things fade. The first few years, I found it quite tough. But life's richer now as a result.

God also had other plans when it came to my career

in scientific research. And it all depends on how you look at it. Some people would (and probably still do) say I was crazy to leave. They'd say I lost job status and security going into Christian ministry. I certainly laid something down; that's true. On the other hand, the work was taking too much love, and I sensed it needed to go. But it did hurt—the first few years, it was almost like a part of me had died. It doesn't always happen this way, but, eventually, when I didn't need it anymore, God gave it back to me in a different shape.

Being that bit older means you can both look back and look forward. I seem to be conscious at the moment that the day will come when I'll have to lay everything in this world down. When I put even my last breath into his hands.

I want to be so used to him and his love being everything that I'm ready for that day when it comes.

He's present with me as I follow him and seek to live like him. He's experienced this journey himself. It's astonishing to be brought right into his ways and his mission. This matters. Finally, real purpose.

It's beautiful and exhilarating to be allowed to partner like this. It'd be too costly and overwhelming, undoable, without his life and power. But this really is partnership. We can test his promises and see.

We pray and depend on his resurrection life, and he works. We share. And where he is, there we will also be (12:26).

Reflection

1. Contemplate John 12:1–33.
2. Being united with Christ changes … Purpose.

How does "me-in-you-and-you-in-me" friendship with Christ shape your idea of purpose and mission? Take some time to talk to him about it now, perhaps praying as in John 14:12–14.

He Makes Alive

"You also will live
because of me."[1]

JOHN 6:57

Life. That word's a big deal for John. And it touches on just about everything in our own minds too. How we react, and what we associate with "life," tends to say a lot. Maybe we're hopeful. Maybe life seems precious but fragile. Or perhaps life feels empty—inescapable, but somehow out of reach.

Wherever you're at with life, you probably feel that if

1   ESV, paraphrased.

we could crack the whole question, we'd be sorted. It's a really big deal.

Jesus agrees. Running water, brilliant light, festivities, fruit, the best wine, all the bread you need. Love that lasts, deep relationships, clear destiny. Jesus' words in John are meant to pulsate with life itself.

I was listening the other day to someone talk about how she encountered Jesus as a student. "I knew something had happened, and Jesus was real to me," she said, "but my biggest fear was that being a Christian would mean being bored and missing out." Now, it hadn't turned out that way for her (we'll see why), but that fear's an interesting one.

Right now, whoever you are, my bet is you're trying to tap into stuff which will make you feel (and keep you feeling) alive, at all sorts of different levels. And you avoid like the plague anything which you reckon might threaten that particular project.

Or else there's a frantic FOMO[2] because you're not quite sure what to choose to tap into.

It might surprise you, but I think Jesus would say that's understandable. He knows how you're put together. He

2   Fear Of Missing Out.

knows what you're made of. He's compassionate. He even stood in your shoes for a while, so he gets it. He knows you need Life.

Life projects

When you consider it, the opposition must be thrilled with the con that following Jesus is dull. Now, trying to imitate Jesus without knowing him and knowing the power of his resurrection, I'll admit *that's* dull. (It's also impossible.) But walking with Jesus has colour, even when the going is tough.

Can I ask you what your life project is? I don't mean what's on your bucket list. I mean what (or who) is life to you.

When I was in my early thirties, my wife and I were sitting in a packed auditorium listening to a very well-known speaker. I don't remember much of the content, but I do recall the topic. It was about how to pinpoint the gods (small "g") that we worship. The things which can still charm us, even as believers.

I'd just landed a big promotion. (That's probably how I'd have put it at the time.) I remember hearing my own voice a lot during the evening, batting away the speaker's challenges (though not out loud!). We filed out with everyone else. My take was that I was underwhelmed. I think we went for a drink, and I spent some time picking potential holes in the arguments.

"Life" sources don't want to die. If you're already firmly plugged into something that doesn't have life in it, it will take quite a lot (maybe a great deal) to change your mind.

Our life projects are well-defended psychologically. They definitely don't want to die. After all, we're relying on them.

The irony about that evening, looking back, was that I'd already invested too heavily in my own career project, and we were about to move city to invest some more. The penny still hadn't properly dropped, though. I had an answer to everything that had been said, or so I thought.

Some parts of the next few years were good, even spiritually life-giving. Jesus is kinder and more patient than I reckoned on back then. But eventually, I was simply forced to admit that I'd pushed the career accelerator as hard to the floor as it was going to go. The career car was going along pretty well. But it wasn't feeling all that great.

After a while, the cars on the motorway don't appear to be moving anymore—plenty of people are going the same way at more or less the same speed. It's unnerving. Maybe you can relate.

The Lord didn't want me to settle.

Real life, real connection

"For as the Father has life in himself, so he has granted the Son also to have life in himself" (John 5:26). There's a god with a big "G." The Father and Son have life in … themselves.

What, then, if the real source of life were to invite you in for connection, personally? What if that kind of life were available in the here and now? And what if "heaven" and deeply experienced love, instead of being different things, were in some ways one and the same?

"And this is eternal life, that they know you, the only true God, and Jesus Christ whom you have sent" (John 17:3). The stuff we all too easily settle for is, frankly, not life. It's important to get that. Heaven is being fully alive. And Jesus' resurrection means that life, eternal life, is breaking in now.[3]

3   Throughout this chapter, I use "heaven" as another word for "eternal life."

If I'd known that evening what being united to Jesus meant, what doors were already open as a result of knowing him, the career door would have seemed like a much smaller deal. I'd have seen it for what it was.

Food that lasts

It's evening again, but in a different place. They're in the middle of nowhere by a massive lake, staring at a boy holding five loaves of bread and two fish. A huge crowd from the surrounding towns has followed Jesus out there. The boy seems to be the only one with any food whatsoever—and there are thousands of people.

"Where are we to buy bread, so that these people may eat?" Jesus asks Philip (John 6:5). We have to eat and drink so regularly, don't we? Stopping to sleep is a necessity. These are reminders that only God has life in himself, and we don't.

Jesus gets them all to sit down on the grass. He knows what he's about to do. He gives thanks over the bread and the fish. Everyone (yes, everybody) eats and is filled, and there are twelve basketfuls of bread pieces left over.

The Son has life in himself.

Unsurprisingly, the people want to make him king by

force, but Jesus withdraws to a place on his own. The next day (after a not-from-this-world night walk in John 6:16–21, again showing Jesus' astonishing power), the crowd go looking for Jesus on the other side of the lake. They reckon Jesus could be a free meal ticket (v. 26)—he rapidly becomes their new economic project.

But Jesus tells them to think bigger. To look for life that lasts, which he can give them. The Israelites in Moses' day ate manna from heaven in the wilderness, but they died. Jesus is talking about a bread from heaven which you can eat and not die (vv. 49–50).

The worst life insurance

Probably everybody dislikes paying for insurance. But we pay it to avoid the possibility of a big loss. We can't cope with the house and everything in it burning down, so we grudgingly sign up for the house insurance. There's a main wage earner for the family, so we reluctantly take out the life insurance.

But imagine this—a life insurance policy that charges plenty of payments but never pays out when someone dies. Obviously, you just wouldn't take out a policy like that.

So, here's an important question: Does the gospel you hear, or the one you've been encouraged to rely on, ever feel like a kind of insurance? The terms of the policy they sell you vary, but the story goes a bit like this.

You sign up to believing in a "creator god," to a sort of morality-for-its-own-sake, and to church attendance on Sundays (of course). If you do well enough, and make enough payment for moral failures, you eventually get some kind of heavenly, eternal existence. It might be rather boring or weird (who knows), but at least death is beaten, and you've avoided something worse. So they tell you.

But this is not Christianity according to Jesus. The policyholder is left guessing all the time what "enough" might be. That hurts. And in reality, there's nobody paying out this way at the end of the day. Eventually, the telltale signs rear their head of someone resenting their faith and trying to obey "just enough but no more."

"How did this ever catch on?" you're tempted to ask. But if we take the personal God out of the picture, the fact is we're left desperate for life and, understandably, terrified of death. And so, the worst insurance policy (ever) often rushes in to fill the vacuum.

Paint the tree

Imagine an artist hired to paint and communicate what a particular tree looks like. (Bear with me, it's a special kind of tree.) As Dane Ortlund puts it, "'Be good' Christianity is not wrong in the way that an artist painting [the] tree across the street and leaving out one of the branches is wrong, but in the way such an artist would be wrong if he had been hired to paint the tree but had chopped it down instead!"[4]

So, instead, let's paint the tree, well … the vine, properly. Let's see it the way the Father and the Son see it.

A branch doesn't sit in a vine to get somewhere else, to a completely different kind of existence. It enjoys life there. For a branch, the vine isn't a means to an end. It's what life is all about, if you see what I mean. The vine's going to flourish over time, so there's no need to fret.

And it should be like that between us and Jesus.

If someone is a means to an end for you, you won't love that person for who she is. (That's true, isn't it?) And as long as we see Jesus as a means to something different, we're missing the beauty of who he is. When we realise he's everything, he becomes the goal, and

4   Ortlund, *Surprised by Jesus*, 59.

"heaven" becomes where he is.

I want to remain in him and his love now, in the vine, because that's where I want to spend eternity. With him.

When you think about it, the vine in John 15 is a vivid picture of life, life which begins here and lasts into eternity. Jesus wants us to be holding onto him (as he holds onto us). Then we realise Jesus and life are the same thing. For a branch, the vine really is life.

It's all about in-one-another love between you and Jesus. No other relationship "makes alive." But this friendship with the Son who has life in himself does exactly that.

Living bread

It's the same in John 6, and it startled the people listening at the time—the bread from heaven which you can eat "and not die" (6:50) turns out to be Jesus himself.

It's another "just as ..." saying. Just as ... Jesus shares the life of the Father and so lives because of the Father—he's in the Father, and the Father is in him—so ... the person who "feeds on" Jesus shares his life and lives because of him (v. 57). You're in the Son, and the Son is in you. His love makes (and keeps) alive, into eternity.

Branches do "feed" off the whole vine (so we can mix our metaphors here). But what kind of feeding does Jesus have in mind? Looking to him and relying on him. Trusting him and relating to him personally. God delights in you as you trust his love:

For this is the will of my Father, that everyone who looks on the Son and believes in him should have eternal life, and I will raise him up on the last day. (John 6:40)

Then, a bit later, Jesus really shocks them. "Looking and believing"—that's trusting—become "feeding on his flesh and drinking his blood" (v. 54). Same idea, but Jesus wants us to rely on what he does for us on the cross, not on ourselves. (He's not talking directly about bread and wine on a Sunday; that's not the main thing here.)

He wants us to lean into his love. To relate to him and trust him for real. You in him and him in you (v. 56). That's vine life.

If someone asks you, six months after you read this book, to sum it up in one line, here's a good one: it's all about me-in-you-and-you-in-me life with Jesus in the vine. Heaven breaking in now (no exaggeration).

I know some people love diagrams and summaries and that sort of thing, and others would rather hear a good story. But here's a summary that might be worth remembering:

being united to Jesus = vine life = heaven breaking in now

And trusting Jesus personally for this is enough for you to know it's yours. He won't let you down (vv. 37–40). He's sufficient. He is your assurance. You've got to love the "whoever" part of this verse: "Whoever feeds on my flesh and drinks my blood abides in me, and I in him" (v. 56).

I asked my wife Kerstin to explain what this perspective on heaven means to her. This is what she said (her words, not mine):

I trusted Jesus from an early age. I believed that he gave me eternal life. But as I got older, my understanding was rather vague—life that carried on forever, life that went on beyond death. My internal sense of what that heavenly life was like was really abstract. Through my twenties, in particular, this vague idea struggled to compete with the very real demands and rewards in the here and now. "Now" seemed more urgent and more relevant.

I found myself struggling to look forward to something that could fuel my faith now and make a difference to the way I lived day by day. The resources I was offered didn't really help because they were so focused on trying to delve into the details of what heaven would or wouldn't be like. Discovering the message of John's Gospel has made a big difference to me.

If "eternal life" is a real and intimate relationship with Jesus, that changes everything. If I am joined to him already, eternal life is actually about that relationship growing, deepening, and blossoming. I know him now (truly, though not fully), and I'll spend eternity discovering more of how wonderful he is. I worship him now, and heaven is a place of never-ending worship in his immediate presence.

As I treasure Jesus now, I am already tasting heaven. This emphasis on relationship has given my faith an immediacy and a joy that puts this world in perspective. Knowing him is the most important thing, and enjoying him is truly motivating. For me, "living in the light of eternity" has become all about pressing into the presence of Jesus, who is the same yesterday, today, and forever.

The bride city

Maybe you've also found yourself wondering what heaven's going to be like. Heaven is being with him, person-to-person. It's being united with him.

Which must mean that heaven starts now.

Don't get me wrong. Plenty about our days here can be anything but easy. There's weakness as well as resurrection power at work. There's suffering as well as tasting God's joy. But heaven, eternal life, is all about being one with Christ. It's vine life beginning for you, and then flourishing beyond your wildest dreams.

Before you wonder if this book has gone a bit wacky, let's ask what John sees in Revelation when he looks at the life to come. Everything being made new (Revelation 21–22). God dwelling with people. Them belonging to him in love. Him wiping away every tear, for good … It's deeply relational.

Now, you've heard of garden cities. But what John sees, when you think about it, is a garden-temple city. (It has the layout of a temple in the vision, and it reminds us of Eden.) The river of the water of life runs through it. The people see God's face. There's no night. The glory of Jesus floods the place. It's all about the presence and friendship of God.

Why isn't John shown all the detail in his vision (assuming we could actually take it in)? There's a lot we might like to know—the vegetarian lions and harmless snakes in Isaiah 11 sound interesting, for a start. But what John sees is what we *need* to know now about where we're headed.

This is the only city which is also a bride. Christ's bride. Heaven is where the Father and the Son live with the people of God, united to them in love. That probably rings a bell (John 14:23). It's all about "me-in-you-and-you-in-me."

So, heaven starts now. It's vine life.

Reflection

1. Read John 6:1–15 and 6:41–59.
2. Being united with Christ changes … Life.

Imagine echoing Jesus' words in John 6:57 and saying,

"I live because of the Son." Perhaps write something down, or talk to him, about the difference that makes. Talk to him about your hope of … Heaven.

He Fathers

> "You will know the truth, and the truth will set you free. … The slave does not remain in the house forever; the son remains forever."

JOHN 8:32, 35

Some people say they feel free when they walk by the crashing waves on a beach. Or hurtle down a snowy mountainside on two planks. Or when they spend a lazy Saturday afternoon with a good friend doing nothing very much at all. I think what they mean is, they feel alive. They feel free to be.

When I look back, I realise I grew up thinking freedom meant freedom to choose. Independent choice.

Now, I can see where that's coming from. Sometimes it's obvious what the best choice would be, if only I (or someone else) could make it happen. But how much of that kind of freedom do you think you could realistically handle? Who do you want to have driving the really important stuff forward?

I suspect there's a deeper longing behind our love of free choice. The longing to feel alive. The freedom to discover where we fit and belong. To do what it feels like we were made for.

If you've read this far, you're not going to be surprised by what I say next: Jesus reckons freedom is linked to something else—belonging.

I've never met anyone who seems as free as Jesus. He's free from fear and the need to impress. Free from futility. Free from being unable to love. Free from not knowing. Sometimes, he does stuff that's free from the so-called "laws" of physics. (He designed the system and the textbook, after all.)

Jesus is free enough to have the strength to lay down his life because he loves you. And his life is one of entwined dependence on the Father: his life is one of "me-in-you-and-you-in-me" fellowship with the Father.

Surprisingly, and strangely to our ears, freedom comes when we discover the right kind of belonging.

My Father ... and your Father!

Have you noticed how knowing a friend sometimes means striking up a friendship with that person's parents too? A friend at college who was a bit older than me got on really well with my dad. All three of us would go to watch the rugby at Twickenham sometimes. And the brother of my best friend (when we were living in Hull) became a lifelong friend of the family and of my dad, especially.

"Me-in-you-and-you-in-me" relationship with Jesus joins you with his Father too. Jesus is *the* Son, and you become a son or a daughter also. You get to depend on the Father and to belong with him in the same way Jesus does. You get to stand in his shoes. I'm not exaggerating here. You find freedom in the Father's embrace.

Knowing Jesus means knowing the Father. And Jesus doesn't just whisper that you're his brother or sister. He writes it large across the pages of the New Testament. He's never ashamed to look you in the eye and say, "You're family" (Heb. 2:11–12). He was made like you in every way (v. 17), to bring you to God.

Mary Magdalene had watched the unwatchable. Early on the Sunday morning (John 20:1), she came to Jesus' tomb, surrounded by darkness still—her heart shaken, her stomach churning.

"Mary." Mary turns and recognises Jesus (v. 16). To her astonishment, her world hasn't ended. They haven't lost him. Even more, his resurrection is going to bring her and them home. They belong to something far bigger than they'd imagined.

Jesus said to Mary, "Go to my brothers and say to them, 'I am ascending to my Father and your Father, to my God and your God.'" So Mary Magdalene went and announced to the disciples, "I have seen the Lord" (vv. 17–18).

This is what vine life, resurrection life, means. When you get out of bed tomorrow morning, you can say, "Jesus' Father is my Father." That's huge. It means that as you walk through tomorrow, you can know Jesus as the King who is also your brother.

God sees himself truly as your Father—you're free to be in his family. The air you breathe is Christ's freedom, the Son's freedom. And the mission we share in is the

Son's mission.

There's a chain reaction going on. The Father sends the Son because he wants to set people free. Jesus shares fully with you and me as family, without holding back. And so he sends us out to spread the same freedom (v. 21).

Held

That evening, Jesus stands among his disciples and breathes on them, saying, "Receive the Holy Spirit." This is beautiful. Sharing the Spirit of the Son, you receive Jesus' commission to take God's forgiveness and freedom to hurting people (John 20:22–23). We're forgiven people who get to help restore those around us to friendship and union with God. We're people who carry the forgiveness which is able to break the grip sin has on things.

When you think about it, all forgiveness is deeply personal—just ask someone struggling to forgive to explain the reasons why. When God forgives you, it's personal between you and him.

And of course, when we're reconciled with someone we've really offended, let back close, it's even better to know that we won't easily lose them again. How much more with God's forgiveness. The love which completely removes the sin and breaks its power, that love now also holds us secure—for keeps.

There's a small picture by Rembrandt (not even twenty centimetres tall) on the windowsill by my desk. I'm looking at it right now. My wife framed this picture and gave it to me years ago, and I've kept it near my desk at home ever since.

The original, *The Return of the Prodigal Son*, stands at over two metres tall in the Hermitage Museum of Saint Petersburg.

One evening, I walked into a city-centre church near where I lived at the time. A huge canvas depicting the same parable, drawn by Charlie Mackesy,[1] hung from floor to ceiling. The son, the younger one in the parable, looked broken and battered. The father's embrace was tender, as well as dependable and strong.

I couldn't take my eyes off the canvas. I'd looked at a different version by my desk for a long time. But it was more than the familiarity. The place where it hung said very clearly, "We've stopped pretending here, and there's a true love that is stronger, a love that can heal."

1   Charlie Mackesy is author of *The Boy, the Mole, the Fox, and the Horse* (London: Ebury Press, 2019).

In Rembrandt's picture, the older son looks on, and looks down, cool and remote. But the father stoops, hands touching and embracing the younger son's shoulders in compassion and healing. Too gentle to harm and too strong to let go. The younger son leans into his father, torn and battered, but totally safe.

The father's heart longs for both his sons to know they belong in the parable of Luke 15. But each son misunderstands the father and the home he wants for them. Jesus' parable is about how you and I bizarrely resist the love, depth of relationship, and freedom that God is offering us.

At the beginning, the younger son just wants his father for the economic blessing he can get out of him. He takes the cash and then runs as far away as he can (vv. 11–16). He'll try anything to fill the void on the inside.

He's never properly understood how his father feels—that's why he ended up leaving. Later, when the going gets tough, he figures his father might have him back as a servant (vv. 17–19). He thinks the father's "forgiveness" might stretch to getting over the past and giving him a chance to earn his way in the future—how could he expect more?

He has more in common with his older brother than we might have thought! The older one blows up at the party which the father throws when the younger son returns home (vv. 25–30). I reckon the older brother's words would have cut deep—he tells his dad that for years he's seen himself simply as a servant, having to obey commands from the top.

So, the older son also wanted his father for the stuff and social status he could get out of him. (I'm guessing that's why he obeyed.) He too missed out on a friendship of love with his father. At this point, you're really starting to feel their father's pain.

But the father still longs for meaningful relationship with them both. He still wants them to know the joy of their home with him as true sons. Free. Valued and loved. He still wants them around the table, eating and enjoying life with him.

And so when the younger son returns, the father literally runs. He embraces and kisses him while he is still a long way away (v. 20). This boy probably couldn't have hurt his father more. He's done his worst, but the father's love for him holds steady. There's deep compassion and forgiveness here.

We don't flit in and out of being sons and daughters of God. As you look to Jesus and the Father forgives you, he unites you to Jesus permanently. He places that eternal robe of sonship on your shoulders. He puts a ring on your finger to let you know you properly belong. And you're held in an embrace you could never have imagined.

When I was a young Christian, I used to think that asking for forgiveness was me asking God to have me back. But now I know that praying for forgiveness is me saying sorry to the One I love for grieving him. It's me telling my Father just how much I want to remain and live where I am in his embrace, loving him back.

Are we willing to be a son or daughter of the Father? Henri Nouwen knows the stakes for freedom can be high:

While God wants [for me] the full dignity of sonship, I keep insisting that I will settle for being a hired servant ... Do I truly want to be so totally forgiven that a completely new way of living becomes possible? Do I want to break away from my deep-rooted rebellion against God and surrender myself so absolutely to God's love that a new person can emerge? Receiving [love and] forgiveness requires a total willingness to let God be God and do all the healing, restoring, and renewing.[1]

I'm praying that a generation of sons and daughters will realise the radical love of the Father for them early on in their lives, know the breath of the Spirit on them, and take this freedom and new life wherever they go.

Belonging and belief

Jesus also talks about who we belong to in John 8. About belief and belonging. About slavery and sonship.

The scary thing is, the people he's talking to reckon that God is already their spiritual Father. They're biological sons. Descendants of Abraham. And they're willing to believe theological stuff about Jesus (8:31). "Surely that's enough?" they say.

It terrifies me that, in the UK, my generation inside the church seem sometimes to have watered down the

1   Henri J. M. Nouwen, *The Return of the Prodigal Son* (London: Darton, Longman, and Todd, 2004), 53.

relational content of the gospel so much. People can end up thinking that "right" belief (orthodoxy) is enough for true life.

But the tragedy is that people need and want true belonging—both those inside the church and those looking on and wondering why they don't see more. They're hungry for a radical love which can set them free.

And that's what Jesus is offering:

If you abide in my word … you will know the truth, and the truth will set you free. … Everyone who commits sin is a slave to sin. The slave does not remain in the house forever; the son remains forever. So if the Son sets you free, you will be free indeed. (John 8:31–36)

Jesus was speaking to people whose identity was their religion, people who were convinced they already belonged to God (v. 41). But they were strangers to the sort of relationship God would want with them as their Father.

People may say they believe, or even say they trust, certain truths about Jesus. But it's a question, Jesus says, of where someone is choosing to make their home.

So he points out to them, "If God were your Father, you would love me" (v. 42). "If you know the Father, if you're at home with him and love him, it'll show in your love for me." That's what Jesus is saying to these people who claim they believe the truth (vv. 54–56).

We've seen the younger brother's dramatic journey from slave to permanent son in Luke 15. These people in John 8 are very like his older brother, aren't they? They're strangers to the Father's embrace. We don't know what happened to the older brother in the parable. But we do know what God's invitation to him sounded like.

It's what God says to us if we find ourselves not identifying as his son or daughter, not at home in the Father's love, and not united to our true Brother. God invites us with deep compassion and understanding into the life and freedom that Jesus the Son has: "Be always with me; know all that is mine is yours" (see Luke 15:31).

It's the invitation to rest in the tender embrace of the Father.

Reflection

1. Read the parable Jesus tells in Luke 15:11–32.

2.   Being united with Christ changes … Freedom.

Contemplate the different characters in Jesus' parable in Luke 15. In what ways do you identify with them? If you find it helpful, consider a picture of Rembrandt's painting *The Return of the Prodigal Son*.

How might you move deeper into experiencing the freedom of loving God as your own Father?

He Invites

"Ask, and you will receive, that
your joy may be full."

JOHN 16:24

"In this day," Jesus says:

> You will know that I am in my Father
> (and my Father is in me)

> You will know that you are in me and I in you

> You will love one another

You will know the Spirit of truth

You will see (and know) me

You will do the works I do

You will live because of me

You will know the truth,
and the truth will set you free!

These eight "you will" sayings of Jesus that we've encountered in John's Gospel go together in our experience as Christians. They describe true life, today—"in this day" following his death and resurrection. Rip out any of them, and what you're left with really isn't life.

The "you will" sayings explain what it means to experience the reality of life in the vine. The reality of worship. The reality of the "me-in-you-and-you-in-me" intimacy with Christ we've been diving into.

There's a ninth "you will" saying which belongs together with the other eight. Jesus says vine life always involves saying "yes" to this. God invites us to ask and receive: "Ask, and you will receive, that your joy may be full" (John 16:24).

Ask to share in, and do, the kind of mission we see Jesus doing in John's Gospel, showing the Father's love. Remember that 14:12–14 kind of prayer? Ask for vine fruit, for the kind of love for people which Jesus has (15:7–9, 16).

When you think about it, this kind of asking means praying to receive and experience more of life in the vine day by day. And Jesus says vine life is joyful (15:11). Full of his own joy!

Because we live in a world that's very often weeping, silently on the inside and loudly on the outside, we get cynical. But Jesus can't just be talking about a joy to be had beyond this world. We've seen that. He's talking about heaven, true life, breaking into this world. About joy breaking in.

You might sometimes wonder how that's possible. Our "you will" sayings help here, because they tie the joy Jesus is talking about to close communion with God. (The nine sayings are a set.) This joy comes from being united to Jesus by the Spirit; that's what has resurrection life breaking in, today.

Jesus says it's a bit like the joy of a baby being born (16:21). Joy coming through and in the midst of struggle. The kind of joy nobody can take away (16:22).

It's probably all too easy to hear these words and say, "Sounds good in theory." But maybe we're still not thinking of quite the right kind of joy and happiness.

What if prayer was an indispensable way to enjoy being one with Jesus? What if prayer was to become so central to our lives that enjoyment of him flowed right in?

I think that's what Jesus is talking about here.

Joy-full

We can sometimes feel swamped by the questions which swirl around in our heads (16:23). But there's a kind of prayer, prayer from that place of "you-in-me-and-me-in-you" connection with God, which puts an end to guesswork and allows life to flow in.

I worry that large sections of the church in the West are misunderstanding or forgetting what prayer is. We're thirsty for joy, and we know it.

In that day you will ask in my name, and I do not say to you that I will ask the Father on your behalf;

for the Father himself loves you, because you have loved me and have believed that I came from God. (John 16:26–27)

That's asking "in Jesus' name" because it's prayer from the place of being united to Jesus and one with him. Asking from the place of being loved by Father, Son, and Spirit. Prayer is the language we use when we're loved by the Son and loving him in return. Prayer is the language of holy love.

Charles Spurgeon speaks poetically about this language of love:

Prayer comes spontaneously from those who abide in Jesus, even as certain oriental trees, without pressure, shed their fragrant gums. Prayer is the natural outgushing of a soul in communion with Jesus. Just as the leaf and the fruit will come out of the vinebranch ... because of its living union with the stem ... so do abiders pray.[1]

---

1   C. H. Spurgeon, *The Metropolitan Tabernacle Sermons*, vol. 34 (London: Passmore & Alabaster, 1855–1860), 14–15.

I wondered this morning how I would feel if, for some bizarre or unimaginable reason, prayer was taken out of the picture. What's the thing I'd miss most? I realised it wasn't being able to ask God to move my circumstances, although I often do, and I'm thankful when he answers and acts. The thing I couldn't get by without is communing with God in prayer. Sharing life with him.

The thing I want to ask for more than anything else is more of *him*.

Praying is, at heart, a vital way of loving God back. And the way we can enjoy and connect with him. That's why one pastor I know talks about "loving God *through* prayer."[2] Sung worship is another way of doing that—prayer with melody and harmony.

Only Jesus can constantly overflow with joy and life. Being one with him means asking to receive more of him! It's a bit like wanting to deepen relationship with a friend. A student put it like this:

In prayer, God … tears down my barriers, fights through my mask, and he moulds me into his

2   Charlie Cleverly, *Epiphanies of the Ordinary: Encounters that Change Lives* (London: Hodder, 2013), 138.

image, shapes my will to his ... Prayer makes my heart vulnerable to God, so that he can place on it whatever he wishes.[3]

There may be many things the Lord wants to put on our hearts in those moments. But a main one is his joy.

If we want to build a friendship or deepen a marriage but always talk at surface level (or don't talk at all), then we know we can't expect much to happen. If we hold ourselves back and don't receive the other person, again, nothing much happens, except some frustration and demotivation.

The place of asking in Jesus' name is the place of participating in the love and joy and presence of the Father and the Son, by the Spirit.

My experience of prayer has changed a lot over the decades. It's become much more about vital relationship. I'll often try to begin simply and remind myself, "I'm in Jesus, and he's in me!" However I might be feeling as I start the day—whether it's pitch black outside or it's a bright, summer morning—that's the spiritual reality as I begin to pray. And it can make all the difference;

3   Cleverly, *Epiphanies of the Ordinary*, 140.

it reminds me there's no barrier between me and God.

Whatever I might be going through, I'm one with Jesus, and that often has reassurance breaking in as I pray. What's more, there are real, spiritual resources I can draw on for the day ahead. Realising prayer is all about "me-in-you-and-you-in-me" friendship and intimacy with Christ changes the whole experience.

I pray knowing God is there. I start to see things from his perspective. As I draw near, I become thrilled by his presence and want to bring him delight as I pray. Prayer becomes part of worship. Sometimes I sit, sometimes I walk around and sing. And if something isn't going to seem relational, from both God's perspective and mine, I try to avoid it. I want to be sharing with Christ and loving God back as I pray.

Relationship with Christ is two-way, and my journey of prayer has been two-way as well. The Spirit really does guide us. Over years of travelling in the close communion of prayer, there's been an asking and receiving which makes up the story and person God is writing me to be. If that sounds unfamiliar, then don't worry: I still want to encourage you to enter into that kind of adventure.

If you look at Jesus' own prayer in John 17 there are, at most, five simple requests. There's so much in this prayer which is a sharing out loud with the Father—a common purpose and plan, a shared knowledge and love.

Christ's power and presence are revealed to us as we journey in prayer in ways that astonish to begin with and then deeply reassure. God responds to you and me in our lives when we seriously take him up on the invitation to pray and ask in Jesus' name.

For years, an older friend and partner in ministry has prayed every day for me. I've had the joy of walking in the obvious answers to her prayer; Gwen has had the joy of partnering with the Lord. And I think the Lord has delighted to see his children share in what he's doing.

God leads you into more

Perhaps you're looking at these "you will" statements, these nine promises of Jesus, and you're aware that you want to dive into a kind of relationship with God you had no idea was possible.

Jesus says, "Come." God's arms are wide open.

Come, everyone who thirsts, come to the waters;
and he who has no money, come, buy and eat …

without money and without price. (Isa. 55:1; see John 4:13–14)

Maybe you're reading these nine "you will" promises, and you're longing for more. It's possible to get confused here, but wanting more is definitely a sign of life.

If that sounds surprising, let's go back to life in the vine, to the relational reality you're already in if you're trusting Jesus. Any wonderful friendship has you wanting to share it more together, doesn't it? Any good marriage has you wanting to live in it more deeply. (Of course, the sort of "more" you want is different when the relationship has already become a reality—you know better what to want.)

Hoping like this is deeply Christian. As we've seen, hoping like this is the hope of heaven, a reality which is breaking in now. There will be both tasting and longing. Knowing and waiting. We wait assured—content as we look to Jesus, but not yet fully satisfied. This is the sort of tension you don't want to see resolved before you're finally face-to-face with him.

One pastor puts it like this:

There is a greater, deeper, closer walk in intimacy, love and joy with our Lord. ... The "more" comes by an intensification of [encounter with] the Spirit within us as our hunger leads to [further] surrender of our ambitions, affections, possessions—everything to His Lordship. Sometimes the more breaks in like a flood, but it may also be an ever-increasing movement into the depths of God's love and power. The more flows out of the finished work of [Christ] and, far from undermining it, further mines it of what Christ won for us.[4]

"Ask, and you will receive, that your joy may be full," Jesus says (John 16:24). "Ask me to know more of the beauty of me-in-you-and-you-in-me."

What does it mean, then, to be full of joy and full of the Spirit? Suppose you're in the supermarket, shopping for a dinner party, and someone says it looks like you have your hands full. They're implying you're near capacity, aren't they? You just can't carry any more bags of good things right now! (Nobody is suggesting you've exhausted the capacity of the supermarket here.)

Being full of joy means having a joy that finds its way

4   Simon Ponsonby, *More* (Colorado Springs: David C. Cook, 2009), 209.

out and overflows. Being filled with the Holy Spirit means receiving from the Spirit in a way that spills over. And as we're filled, our capacity grows too.

Ask – receive – be filled – love – grow – ask …

It's part of the dynamic of "me-in-you-and-you-in-me" intimacy with Christ. God invites you into more.

Reflection

1. Consider John 16:5–28.
2. Being united with Christ changes … Prayer.

Ponder the kind of shape your times of prayer tend to take currently. In what ways might prayer from the place of "me-in-you-and-you-in-me" friendship with Christ develop in future for you?

Take some time now to dwell on the phrases *loving God through prayer* and *relational prayer*.

God
Embraces

The "me-in-you-and-you-in-me" love of God really is a love that joins and marries you to Christ.

And it's not just John who tells us about how Jesus and believers are one. Here are some words from Paul too: "He who is joined to the Lord becomes one spirit with him" (1 Cor. 6:17); and

For no one ever hated his own flesh, but nourishes and cherishes it, just as Christ does the church, because we are members of his body. "Therefore a man shall leave his father and mother and hold fast to his wife, and the two shall become one flesh." This mystery is profound, and I am saying that it refers to Christ and the church. (Eph. 5:29–32)

As we've seen, this is a mystery that's deep and that is knowable now, because Jesus is raised and ascended. It's a love for all. It's a love equally for single and married people.

Paul tells us human marriage can point us to something beyond itself. So we're going to imagine a marriage story, one that's similar in some ways to Jesus' parable in Luke 15.

Amelia has suddenly left her relationship with Theo, who has been courting her. Theo loves her—as much as he loves himself, in fact. But Amelia struggled to trust him and be close to him; she doesn't really know how he's always felt about her. So Theo goes out to find her from his father's farm, where Amelia had been working. When he sees her, she is broken and messed up.

Amelia's feeling totally isolated. She reckons she might still have to work for Theo's father, just to make ends meet. Any chance of marriage seems gone. But that evening, Theo returns with her to the farm and makes sure she has what she needs. The next morning, she's able to take a bath and get ready to have some breakfast. She eats and then goes for a walk. Theo surprises her with gifts of the kind of clothes and jewellery she likes. And there are no reprisals. There's no guilt trip. His love for her always holds steady.

And then he sees that Amelia is starting to love him back too.

The weeks pass … and there's an engagement. An embrace that takes her breath away. An engagement that can't be lost. The two become one.

Christ loves you and me, personally! He goes out to find us because he values us. He wins our hearts. This is the way he relates to us. Being united to the Son now means you're held, forever, in that "me-in-you-and-you-in-me" embrace with him.

~

We're going to finish with a blast from the past. In seventeenth-century England, lots of ministers were cruelly persecuted and then kicked out of the churches where they served. What helped them to get through was this:

the personal, lover-like passion of Christ—what they called the "spiritual marriage"—specifically for each one of them as an individual believer, loved with all of the madness in Christ's soul.[1]

That's the difference the resurrection of Jesus made then. And it's the difference the resurrection of Jesus makes today. Jesus loves you into true life.

God is able to hold you with his love, strongly and tenderly, in this "me-in-you-and-you-in-me" embrace. Many across the world today are finding God's closeness there to be a spiritual reality—one with Christ.

That's thrilling and beautiful. It captures all the priorities and desires of your heart. Heaven is breaking in. Christ is near, to stay. It's the place of true freedom, worship, and prayer. Two-way love. *One*.

~

**Being united to Jesus really does change …
everything. Yes, everything!**

1   Julian Hardyman, *Jesus, Lover of My Soul* (London: Inter-Varsity Press, 2020), 166.

ACKNOWLEDGEMENTS

Each of us is involved in ministry of some kind. Whatever that ministry may be, it's not our own. It's the Lord's, and it's the love and work of many people in his body. Wonderfully, we get to share it and join in!

I can't trace all the ways that others have contributed to this book. I'm grateful for all of you. Thank you to Kerstin, for reading many drafts and for galvanising me to write something from the heart. Thank you to Matt, for wonderful discussions about writing and the life of worship. Thank you to my pastor, Tom, and to Grace Community Church. Thank you to friends at Union, who have encouraged me often and acted as a sounding board, and to the great team at Union Publishing. And thank you to Eleanor, my editor, for urging me early on "to think outside the box" and for being a trusted discussion partner in the ups and downs of the creative process. This book would not have happened without you all.

FURTHER READING

Clive Bowsher, *Life in the Son: Exploring Participation and Union with Christ in John's Gospel and Letters*. Downers Grove: Inter-Varsity Press and London: Apollos, 2023.

This book explores oneness with Christ in John's Gospel and letters in greater theological depth.

Julian Hardyman, *Jesus, Lover of My Soul*. London: Inter-Varsity Press, 2020.

This book encourages you to live a life of worship, prayer and love which takes hold of the reality of being united to Jesus.

Peter Mead, *Lost in Wonder: A Biblical Introduction to God's Great Marriage*. Fearn, Ross-shire, Scotland: Christian Focus, 2016.

This book helps you see and enjoy the theme of God's union and marriage with his people, through the whole of Scripture.

SCRIPTURE INDEX

6:41–49	101	14:8	16
6:49–50	93	14:9–10	16
6:50	96	14:10	15, 35
6:54	97	14:10–11	20
6:56	98	14:11	78
6:57	87, 97, 102	14:11–12	79
8:31–32	24	14:12	73
8:21–36	113	14:12–14	78, 79, 80,
8:31	112		85, 119
8:32	103	14:14	81
8:35	103	14:15	45, 68, 83
8:41	113	14:15–17	67
8:42	114	14:15–24	68
8:54–56	114	14:15–31	71
10:30	17	14:16–17	64, 68
10:38	17	14:17	59, 60, 64
12:1–2	73	14:18	62, 65, 68
12:1–33	85	14:18–21	67
12:3	74	14:19–20	67
12:4–6	74	14:20	12, 15, 27,
12:7	75		31, 33
12:23	75	14:21	53, 68
12:24–26	81	14:23	53, 62, 65,
12:25	82		68, 101
13:1	18	14:23–24	68
13:34	81	14:27	62
13:35	18	15:1	32
14:1	62	15:1–12	34, 44
14:2	62	15:2	34
14:1–11	25	15:3	34
14:2–5	61	15:4	51
14:3	61	15:5	32, 35
14:6–7	19	15:6	51
14:7	16	15:7	51, 53, 60

Union
AUTHENTIC MINISTRY
SERVING FROM
THE HEART
MICHAEL REEVES

GIVEAWAY

RECEIVE FREE
RESOURCES EVERY
MONTH WHEN YOU
SUBSCRIBE TO
UNION PUBLISHING.

UP